DISCOVERING BIBLICAL TREASURES

# UNDERSTANDING ENOCH'S VIEW OF HEAVEN

A STUDY OF THE BOOK OF THE WATCHERS
1 ENOCH CHAPTER 17 TO 36
USING ANCIENT BIBLE STUDY METHODS

**Michael Harvey Koplitz**

Editor, contributor, and facilitator: Rabbi Rev. Dr. Michael H. Koplitz, D.Min., Ph.D.

Contributors: Sandra Koplitz, Linda Hivner, Michael Hivner

First edition 2019



The Book of the Watchers text from 1 Enoch: The Hermeneia Translation Paperback – October 1, 2012, by George W. E. Nickelsburg (Author), James C. Vanderkam (Author)

Published by Michael H. Koplitz

# Table of Contents

# INTRODUCTION

This work is the collective wisdom of a class of students who were studying the Book of the Watchers from 1 Enoch. Pastor Michael Koplitz, who authored this document and did the basic research, led the class. The class was conducted using Ancient Bible Study methods, which were employed by the people of the first century C.E. This study lasted over three years. The Book of the Watchers is quoted in the Christian Scriptures, and it is clear from archeological discoveries that early Jewish-Christians were reading this book.

The church was reading 1 Enoch until a Pope of the church banned it in the seventh century C.E. However, that did not stop people from learning from this book. That a fallen angel became Satan is found in the Book of the Watchers. The rabbis who met at Yamnia around 90 C.E. wanted to include this book in the Bible. The objection was that the book could not be found in Hebrew. The rabbis had determined that only writings that were written in Hebrew had the true blessing of the LORD. Since 1 Enoch has only been discovered, thus far, in Aramaic and Coptic, it became a part of the Pseudepigrapha.[1]

By studying the Book of the Watchers, one can learn how sin and evil came into our world and how we can permanently, if possible, completely remove evil. If not from the world, then from within us.

If the reader is not familiar with Ancient Bible study methods, it is recommended that the articles about this study method be read. After reading the article, enjoy the wisdom the LORD has placed upon this study group.

---

[1] spurious or pseudonymous writings, especially Jewish writings ascribed to various biblical patriarchs and prophets but composed within approximately 200 years of the birth of Jesus Christ.

This is the second half of the Book of the Watchers. In the second half, Enoch is taken on a tour of heaven. Remember that Enoch wrote what he saw in heaven using physical terms.

## THE MAIN DIFFERENCES BETWEEN THE GREEK METHOD OF TEACHING AND THE HEBRAIC METHOD

Once you are aware of the two teaching styles, you will determine if you are in a class or reading a book, whether the analysis and teaching method is in a Greek or Hebraic method. In the Greek method, the instructor is right because of advanced knowledge. In the college situation, it is because the professor has his/her Ph.D. in some area of study, so one assumes that he or she knows everything about the topic. For example, Rodney Dangerfield played the role of a middle-aged man going to college. His English midterm was to write about Kurt Vonnegut Jr. Since he did not understand any of Vonnegut's books, he hired Vonnegut himself to write the midterm. When it was returned to him, the English Professor told Dangerfield that whoever wrote the paper knew nothing about Vonnegut. This is an example of the Greek method of teaching. Did the Ph.D. English professor think she knew more about Vonnegut's writings than Vonnegut did? [2]

In the Greek teaching method, the professor or the instructor claims to be the authority. If you are attending a Bible study class and the class leader says, "I will teach you the only way to understand this biblical book," you may want to consider the implications. This method is common since most Seminaries and Bible colleges teach a Greek method of learning, which is the same method the church has been utilizing for centuries.

Hebraic teaching methods are different. The teacher wants the students to challenge what they hear. It is through questioning that a student can learn. Also, the

---

[2] *Back to School*. Performed by Rodney Dangerfield. Hollywood: CA: Paper Clip Productions, 1986. DVD.

teacher wants his/her students to excel to a point where the student becomes the teacher.

It is said that if two rabbis come together to discuss a passage of Scripture, the result will be at least ten different opinions. All points of view are acceptable if biblical evidence can support the points. It is permissible and encourages students to have multiple opinions. There is a depth to God's Word, and God wants us to find all His messages that are placed in the Scriptures.

Seeking the meaning of the Scriptures beyond the literal meaning is essential to fully understand God's Word.[3] The Greek method of learning the Scriptures has prevailed over the centuries. One problem is that many often viewed only the literal interpretation of Scripture as valid, influenced by Martin Luther's "sola literalis" which meant that only the literal interpretation of Scripture was valid. The Fundamentalist movements of today are generally based on the literal interpretation of the Scripture. Therefore, they do not believe that God placed any deeper, hidden, or secret meanings in the Word.

The students of the Scriptures who learn through Hebraic training and understanding have drawn a different conclusion. The Hebrew language itself leads to different possible interpretations because of the construction of the language. The Hebraic method of Bible study opens avenues of thought about God's revelations in the Scripture that may have never been considered. A question may be raised about the Scripture being studied for which there may not be an immediate answer. If so, it becomes the responsibility of the learners to uncover the meaning. Also, remember that multiple opinions about the meaning of Scripture are also acceptable if they can be supported by Scripture.

---

[3] Davis, Anne Kimball. *The Synoptic Gospels*. MP3. Albuquerque: NM: BibleInteract, 2012.

## AN UNDERSTANDING OF HEBRAIC THOUGHT IN BIBLE STUDY

We should start this discussion by asking, "Why does a reader of the Bible need to understand Hebraic thought?" When we read most commentaries about the Bible, we listen to the TV pastors, the famous speakers, or even our local church pastors, who tell us how to understand the Bible, but they rarely mention Hebraic thought.

There is a difference between Greek/Western thought and Hebraic thought. It is amazing how many people, including many educated pastors and seminary professors, think Christianity is a western religion. The origin of Christianity is Hebraic! Jesus was a trained rabbinical Jew who ministered around the Sea of Galilee and Judea doing what rabbis do best – interpreting the Hebrew Scriptures. The original twelve disciples of Jesus Christ were all Jewish. They thought Jewish, they lived Jewish, their culture was Jewish, and many authors of the New Testament were Jewish. Hebraic storytelling and parables are contained in the Bible. Whether you examine the Old Testament (which will now be referred to as the Hebrew Scriptures) or the New Testament (which will now be referred to as the Christian Scriptures), you are reading Hebraic documents that were composed with Hebraic thought.

Over the past 1900+ years, Christianity has been separated from its mother religion Judaism and has transformed itself into a different religion. We admit that the understanding of the Scriptures within most of the church members today has become a Greek/Western interpretation. When Christianity broke away from Judaism, it lost and forgot its Hebraic roots.[4]

---

[4] Davis, Anne Kimball. *First Century Methods I: Recovering Ancient Methods of Bible Study – Course.* Albuquerque: NM: BibleInteract, 2015.

When a Bible student understands the Hebraic way of thinking the Scriptures will be opened to a deeper understanding and the blessings God offers to His people will become more abundant. A Hebraic view of the Bible reveals a depth of scriptural perception that is amazing. The richness of Scripture is as deep as God is infinite. A passage of Scripture can be read time and time again. Each time one can receive more of what God is revealing. This is the Hebraic process of understanding that there is a rich depth of revelation that God wants to reveal. Consider the Scripture like an onion. It has many layers. As you learn about the outer layer of God's revelation in His Word, God reveals the next layer. This increasing depth of understanding continues for a lifetime. There is an infinite number of insights in the Bible because of God infinite.

Let us start with the basic principles of studying the Scriptures. The first thing is to understand a verse or passage's context.[5] This requires more than just reading the verses before and after the passage being studied. The first seven refer to the history and culture of the people; the last two address the text. The following questions need to be asked:[6]

1. Who is the author?
2. When did the author live?
3. What time is the author writing about?
4. What is the author's point of view?
5. What was the cultural and historical setting at the time the writing was done?
6. Who was the audience the author was writing to?
7. What language was used?
8. What is the plain meaning of the passage?

---

[5] Dye, Diana. *Study to Show Yourself Approved.* Albuquerque: NM: BibleInteract, 2014.

[6] Several question in the list from: Diana Dye. Also from: Boman, Thorleif. *Hebrew Thought Compared with Greek.* Philadelphia: Westminster Press, 1960.

9. What are the presented details? What details are missing?

Unfortunately, there are many modern-day Christian authors today who take single verses out of the Bible and use them in narrow ways to prove or disprove their point of view. This is an incorrect method of utilizing God's Word. The context of the Bible must be understood to comprehend what God is saying. Answering the questions presented above will help establish the context of the passage.

"What is the inner world of biblical thought? What is the cultural mindset of the authors of Holy Writ? Are we to understand the Bible chiefly through the eyes of Hellenism (Greek/Western thought and culture) or through the eyes of Judaism (Hebrew thought and culture)?" [7] A modern example is when a newspaper article from one city in the U.S. is read in another city. If the reader in the other city is not aware of the urban problems of the city, the article is addressed, then the article will be read out of context and its true meaning missed. Understanding the environment of the author is important in understanding what is written.

Paul's letters are a large part of the Christian Scriptures. Today, people interpret these letters as a Christian document. However, Paul was a pious Jew. When these letters are viewed as being written by a Messianic Jew, the theology of Paul expresses becomes clear. "Paul upheld the goodness of the Jewish tradition of the Bible. Indeed, Paul came to understand the Christian life as patterned after that of Judaism." [8] Paul used Hebraic literary devices in his writings, such as Midrash, echoes, and chiasms. When reading Paul's letters, care needs to be taken to look for these literary devices because these linguistic tools will give a correct interpretation of what Paul was trying to say.

---

[7] Wilson, Marvin R. *Our Father Abraham: Jewish Roots of the Christian Faith.* Grand Rapids, MI: W.B. Eerdmans, 1989. 5.
[8] IBID, p. 8.

"If Hebrew thinking is to be characterized, it is obvious first to call it dynamic, vigorous, passionate and sometimes quite explosive in kind; correspondingly Greek thinking is static [harmonic or resting], peaceful and moderate." [9] The Word of God is a dynamic and mighty document. When you read Genesis 1, the creation story, you quickly discover that all of God's creation occurred by God speaking it. "And God said…" Black Fire on White Fire is what the sages call the Torah. The Black Fire is the ink that is used to write the words of the Torah, and the White Fire is the parchment it is written on.[10] When a Torah scroll is worn out, becoming unusable, a funeral service, with a small casket, is held for the scroll that contains the living Word of God.

When God speaks, God acts. This concept has been applied to a person's word that must be translated into a person's actions. "Hebraically, such a concept of pronouncing a word without following it up with actions makes the word null, void, and meaningless." [11] God created the Hebrew language not only so God could communicate with us but also, so God's people could communicate with Him. Therefore, Hebrew is a sacred language. Around 200 B.C.E. Aramaic became the common language outside the Temple and the Synagogue. It was not until the 20th century that Hebrew was revived as a publicly spoken language.[12] For 2100 years Hebrew was a language spoken only in the synagogue while worshiping God.

Hebraic thought views God to have a personality. For example, God is a loving God. In the Hebrew Scriptures, God is described as a warrior, judge, provider, and creator.

---

[9] Boman, Thorleif. *Hebrew Thought Compared with Greek.* Philadelphia: Westminster Press, 1960.
[10] "Rojtman, Betty. *Black Fire on White Fire: An Essay on Jewish Hermeneutics, from Midrash to Kabbalah.* Berkeley: University of California Press, 1998.
[11] Boman, Thorleif. *Hebrew Thought Compared with Greek.* Philadelphia: Westminster Press, 1960.
[12] Fellman, Jack. *The Revival of a Classical Tongue; Eliezer Ben Yehuda and the Modern Hebrew Language.* The Hague: Mouton, 1973.

"To the Hebrew mind, everything is theological. That is, the Hebrews make no distinction between the sacred and the secular areas of life. They saw all of life as unity. It is all God's domain. God has a stake in all that comes to pass."

The sacred and secular areas of life for Jews in Yeshua's day were intertwined, and everything was in God's domain. [13] Hebraic prayers were then and are today short and to the point. Every aspect of life was celebrated in prayer and thanksgiving to God.

Genesis 5:24 and 6:9 tell us that both Enoch and Noah walked with God. The objective of a Jew is to walk with God. To live a life walking with God requires the study of the Torah and obeying every aspect of the Torah, which gives the direction and guidance needed to remain on the way."[14]

Concerning the Scriptures, Hebraic thinking tells us there are no contradictions and certainly no errors in the Bible. Narratives that seem to be repetitive are also in the Word for a specific reason. Our task through life is to learn and study the Bible, so God's revelation can be revealed to us.

There is no one way to interpret Scripture. The idea of discussion, questioning, and debating the meaning of Scripture is a major part of Jewish thought in Bible study. Also, the teacher is not considered to have the absolute truth of interpretation that is reserved for God. We can only stretch, and stretch some more, to uncover an increasing depth of meaning.

---

[13] Wilson, Marvin R. *Our Father Abraham: Jewish Roots of the Christian Faith*. Grand Rapids, MI: W.B. Eerdmans, 1989.156.

[14] IBID. 160.

## AN UNDERSTANDING OF GREEK THOUGHT IN BIBLE STUDY

Plato's Academy was the forerunner of the modern university system in existence today.[15] Today's Seminaries and Bible Colleges are part of the modern university system and are using the method Plato and his contemporaries employed to view the universe. This Greek system of learning and understanding is also part of our current education system. Therefore, we have been taught that when a teacher, considered an expert in his or her field of study, tells us something, we must accept it without question. When exam time comes, the students are expected to repeat what the teacher has said whether they agree with it.

The same occurs in church when the pastor follows the Greek teaching method he/she was taught in Bible College and Seminary. The pastor offers a sermon or Bible study, and the people sit passively and are expected to agree with the pastor. There is limited dialogue or discussion allowed because the pastor or the presenter is perceived as correct.

In the Greek mindset, hermeneutics is a science, and science proves one way of viewing the world. "Hermeneutics is the study of the methodological principles of interpretation. To interpret the Bible means to understand the Bible." [16] There is a single answer to every question. Of course, today, chaos theory and quantum physics are turning the scientific community somewhat upside down because there can be more than one answer to a question at the subatomic level of matter. Greek thinking is static because once you have interpreted a passage of Scripture, you never have to study it again because you already have the answer.

---

[15] Howland, Jacob. *Plato and the Talmud.* Cambridge: Cambridge University Press, 2011. 130.

[16] Trimm, J. *Hermeneutics: How to Understand the Scripture.* Hurst:Texas: Society for the Advancement of Nazarene Judaism, 2000. 4.

"Thomas Aquinas (1225–1274) lived at a critical juncture of western culture when the arrival of the Aristotelian *corpus* in Latin translation reopened the question of the relation between faith and reason, calling into question the *modus vivendi* that had used for centuries."[17] In simpler words, Aquinas reintroduced the need to study the Scriptures in a Greek manner. Since hermeneutics is viewed as a science, the specific methodology can be used to determine the interpretation of Scripture. In this mindset, everything in the Scripture must be explainable in some way. When a passage cannot be explained, then the idea of errors in the Bible emerged. Perhaps there are passages in the Scriptures that God has made so complex that they cannot be easily understood. Instead of digging for a depth of meaning, the Greek thinker often offers a "non-biblical" explanation.

Many of the basic assumptions and methods of the great Greek thinkers were incorporated into Christianity. When the church decided to leave its Hebraic roots, the methods of thinking were replaced by Greek methods of thought. Since few Jews were becoming believers in Yeshua, the Hebraic methods of Bible study were lost to Christianity.

The Reformation of the church in the 16th century promoted restoration of the original meaning to the Scriptures but did not go to the Jewish roots of the faith. So, the Reformers discouraged debate from being a part of understanding Scripture. They did the same thing they accused the Catholic Church leadership of doing. The Reformers developed a new understanding of the Scriptures and only their conclusions were allowed. This can be seen in the Protestant church today through the numerous

[17] "Aquinas." In *Stanford Encyclopedia of Philosophy*, 1-5. Stanford, CT: Stanford University, Metaphysics Research Lab., 2004. Accessed August 01, 2016. http://plato.stanford.edu/entries/aquinas/.

confessions of faith statements. Each denomination claims the authority of its interpretation.

When the ideas of emotion and passion are taken out of the Scriptures, the Scriptures become Greek. What is left is reason and logic. When you take debate and dialogue out of the equation of understanding the Bible, the ability to understand that the Scripture has a depth of interpretation and understanding is removed.
Analyzing Scripture in this Greek methodology is like putting God in a box. One size fits all. This is not what God intended for His Word. The Bible is a living document which offers many different revelations and depth.

# METHODOLOGY

The method employed is to use First Century Scripture study methods integrated with the customs and culture of Yeshua's day to examine the Hebrew and Christian Scriptures, thus gathering a deeper understanding by learning the Scriptures in the way the people of Yeshua's day did.

In the typical Rabbinic tradition, I had two study partners. Each one served a different function by looking at the research as I put it together. Rev. Dr. Robert Cook, D. Min., an ordained Elder in the United Methodist Church, has been a study partner in different areas of theology and church leadership. He became interested in Hebraic studies when I started sharing Zohar and Midrash with him. He also completed the entire Disciple program as a student and teacher. My second study partner is my wife, Sandra Koplitz, MS. Sandy and I took the instruction class on teaching the Disciple Bible study program, and she takes part in the Zohar study group. Sandy is a licensed local pastor in the United Methodist Church.

## The Process of Discovery

I have titled the method of analyzing a passage of Scripture in a Hebraic manner the "Process of Discovery." This method was developed by the author bringing together the various areas of linguistic and cultural understanding. There are several sections to the process, and not all the sections apply to every passage of Scripture. The overall result of developing this process is to give the reader a framework into the ideas being presented.

The "Process of Discovery" starts with a Scripture passage. If the passage is in a poetic form, it is identified. Possible poetic techniques include parallelism, chiastic structures, and repetition. Formatting the passage in its poetic form allows the reader to visualize what the first century C.E. listener was hearing. Any parallelism is indicated with colored text, and the chiasms are labeled by their corresponding sections, for example A, B, C, B', A'. Not all passages of the Scriptures have a poetic form.

The next step is to "question the narrative," which is accomplished by assuming the reader knows nothing about the passage. Therefore, the questions go from the simple to the complex. The next task is to identify any linguistic patterns. Linguistic patterns include, but are not limited to irony, simile, metaphor, symbolism, idioms, hyperbole, figurative language, personification, and allegory.

Any translation inconsistencies discovered between the English NASB version and either the Hebrew or Greek versions are identified. Sometimes a Hebrew or Greek word can be translated in more than one way. Inconsistencies also can be created by the translation committee, which may have used traditional language instead of the actual translation. The decision of the translation committee can be found in the Preface or Introduction to the Bible. Perhaps some inconsistencies were intentionally added to convey some deeper meaning; therefore, the inconsistencies need to be examined.

Echoes of the Hebrew Scriptures in the Christian Scriptures are identified. This occurs when a passage from the Hebrew Scripture is used in the Christian Scriptures or when a command is directly discussed in the Christian Scriptures. [18] Also, echoes can be found when Torah (Genesis through Deuteronomy) passages are used in other

[18] Mitzvot are the 613 commandments found in the Torah that please God. There are positive and negative commandments. The list was first development by Maimonides. The full list can be found at: ttp://www.jewfaq.org/613.htm.

Hebrew Bible books. Besides echoes, cross-references are listed. A cross-reference is a reference to another verse in the Scripture which can assist the reader in understanding the verse that is being read.

The names of people mentioned in the passage are listed. Many of the Hebrew names have meaning and may be associated with places or actions. Jewish parents used to name their children based on what they felt God had in store for their child. An example of this is Abraham, whose original name was Abram and was changed to mean eternal father (in this case Abram's name was changed by God to Abraham, showing a function he was to perform). When the Hebrew Bible gives names, many of the occurrences will show something special to the reader/listener. The same importance can be held for the names of places. The time to travel between places can supply insight into the event.

Keywords are identified in a verse when they are important to an understanding of that passage. There are no rules for selecting the keywords. Searching for other occurrences of the keywords in Scripture in a concordance is necessary to understand how the word was being used; this must be done in either Hebrew or Greek, not in English. A classic Hebraic approach is to find the usage of a word in the Scripture by finding other verses that contain the word. The usage of a word, in its original language, is discovered by searching for the Scripture in the word's language. The verses that contain the word being researched are identified, and a pattern for the usage of the word is discerned. Each verse is examined to see what the usage of the word is which, may reveal a pattern for the word's usage. For Hebrew words, the first usage of the word in the Scripture, especially if used in the Torah, is important. For the Greek words, the Christian Scriptures are used to determining the word usage in the Scripture.

Sometimes finding the equivalent Greek word in the Septuagint and then analyzing its usage in Hebrew can be very helpful.

The Rules of Hillel for Bible understanding can be used when applicable. Hillel was a Torah scholar who lived shortly before Yeshua's day. Hillel developed several rules for Torah students to interpret the Scriptures which are referred to as halachic Midrash. In several cases, these rules are helpful in the analysis of the Scripture.

After the linguistic analysis is complete, an examination of cultural implications will be examined. The culture is important because it is not specifically referenced in the biblical narratives, as indicated earlier.

From linguistic analysis and cultural understanding, it is possible to get a deeper meaning of the Scripture beyond the literal meaning of the plaintext. That is what the listeners of Yeshua's time were doing. They put linguistics and the culture together without even having to contemplate it. They did it.

This will lead to a conclusion or a set of conclusions about what the passage is discussing. Most of the time, the Hebraic analysis leads to the desire for a deeper analysis to fully understand what Yeshua was discussing or what was happening to Him. Whatever the result, a new deeper understanding of the Scripture will be obtained.

The components of the Process of Discovery are:

- Linguistics Section
  - Linguistic Structure of the Scripture
  - Discussion
  - Questioning the Passage

(Answers to these questions are offered for discussion and you may have different answers. Remember, answers must be defendable from Scripture. Moreover, you may have additional questions about the passage that is not covered. This applies to this section and to the Questioning the Passage in the Cultural section.)

- Main/Center Point
- Verse Comparison of citations or proof text
- Idioms
- Metaphors
- Symbols
- Translation inconsistencies
- People's names
- Name of places
- Word Study
- Topics
- Scripture cross references
- Echoes
- Rules of Hillel

Culture Section

- Discussion
- Questioning the passage culturally

Culture and Linguistics Section

- Discussion

## READING THE SCRIPTURES IN ENGLISH

When you read the Hebrew Scriptures or the Christian Scriptures in English, you are reading a commentary that has three layers.[19] Let us look at why this statement is true.

Starting with Hebrew, we discover that the Hebrew Language is composed of 22 written letters. Biblical Hebrew (and written modern Hebrew in many cases) had no written vowels. Vowel sounds were added by the point system after 600 C.E. to help readers of the Scriptures grasp the words. That means the Masoretes, who created and added vowel points to the Scriptures, did so as they saw fit.

Biblical Hebrew does not have punctuation. Linguistic markers show where sentences begin and end, but someone must determine the format. What word in English offers the best translation for the Hebrew word? A translation committee had to make that determination.

Greek is a little different in that there are vowels, but Koine Greek (common Greek in the ancient world), which the authors of the Christian Scriptures used, has not been a living spoken language for over eighteen centuries. Also, since Koine Greek has no spaces between the words, someone had to determine where spaces should be added to create separate words.

Koine Greek does not have punctuation, so, like Hebrew, you cannot be sure where the sentences begin and end. The same translation problem for Koine Greek to English exists as in Hebrew to English. Someone had to determine the correct sentence structure.

---

[19] During a visit to a synagogue this understanding of the English Bible was offered by Rabbi Jack P. Paskoff, Shaarai Shomayim Congregation, Lancaster, PA. October 2001.

In just about every English translation, except for the King James version, the Bible will have a Preface or Introduction, which is important to read because the translation committee usually explains how the translation was done. It is critical to any Bible study to have a translation that is as close as possible to the original language. Unless you can read Hebrew and Koine Greek, you must rely on the judgment of the English translation committee.

There are some good software packages which can assist you in reading the Bible in its original language. For example, BibleWorks[20] is excellent for the academic study of the Bible. Logos [21] is excellent for laypeople.

When reading a document in English that was originally in Aramaic the commentary levels are equivalent to the Hebrew commentary levels described earlier.

---

[20] BibleWorks 10 Software for Biblical Exegesis Research. Computer software. Version 10. Norfolk, VA: 2014.
[21] Logos Bible Software for Biblical Exegesis Research. Computer Software. Verse 6. Bellingham, WA: 2015.

## ABBREVIATIONS

Bibleworks V10[22] was used for the Scriptures used in this study guide. Below are the abbreviations used in the software.

| **Pentateuch** | GEN | EXO | LEV | NUM | DEU |
|---|---|---|---|---|---|
| **Historical & Poetic** | JOS<br>1KI<br>NEH ECC | JDG<br>2KI<br>EST<br>SOL | RUT<br>1CH<br>JOB | 1SA<br>2CH<br>PSA | 2SA<br>EZR<br>PRO |
| **Prophets** | ISA<br>HOS<br>MIC<br>ZEC | JER<br>JOE<br>NAH<br>MAL | LAM<br>AMO<br>HAB | EZE<br>OBA<br>ZEP | DAN<br>JON<br>HAG |
| **Gospels** | MAT | MAR | LUK | JOH | ACT |
| **Paul** | ROM<br>PHI<br>2TI | 1CO<br>COL<br>TIT | 2CO<br>1TH<br>PHM | GAL<br>2TH | EPH<br>1TI |
| **Apostles** | HEB<br>2JO | JAM<br>3JO | 1PE<br>JUD | 2PE<br>REV | 1JO |
| **Apocrypha** | 1ES<br>3MA<br>PSS<br>PRA<br>JDT<br>4MA | BAR<br>PRM<br>TOB<br>ODE<br>EPJ<br>PSX | 1MA<br>WIS<br>SUS<br>4ES<br>2MA<br>SIP | SIR<br>BEL<br>LAO<br>ESG<br>JSA<br>JDA | TBS<br>SUT<br>DAT<br>BET<br>DNG |

The following is a list of aliases for BibleWorks book name abbreviations. See the Book Names section of the Options window for details on how to add to or change these aliases.

[22] "Bible Version Abbreviations." *Abbreviations.* N.p., n.d. Web. 29 Oct. 2016.

| Internal Name | Name used i n Browse Window | Name used in Exported Verse Lists | Alias 1 | Alias 2 |
|---|---|---|---|---|
| Gen | Genesis | Gen. | Gen | Genesis |
| Exo | Exodus | Exod. | Exo | Exodus |
| Lev | Leviticus | Lev. | Lev | Leviticus |
| Num | Numbers | Num. | Num | Numbers |
| Deu | Deuteronomy | Deut. | Deu | Deuteronomy |
| Jos | Joshua | Jos. | Jos | Joshua |
| Jdg | Judges | Jdg. | Jdg | Judges |
| Rut | Ruth | Ruth | Rut | Ruth |
| 1Sa | 1 Samuel | 1 Sam. | 1Sa | 1Samuel |
| 2Sa | 2 Samuel | 2 Sam. | 2Sa | 2Samuel |
| 1Ki | 1 Kings | 1 Ki. | 1Ki | 1Kings |
| 2Ki | 2 Kings | 2 Ki. | 2Ki | 2Kings |
| 1Ch | 1 Chronicles | 1 Chr. | 1Ch | 1Chronicles |
| 2Ch | 2 Chronicles | 2 Chr. | 2Ch | 2 Chronicles |
| Ezr | Ezra | Ezr. | Ezr | Ezra |
| Neh | Nehemiah | Neh. | Neh | Nehemiah |
| Est | Esther | Est. | Est | Esther |
| Job | Job | Job | Job | Job |
| Psa | Psalm | Ps. | Psa | Psalm |
| Pro | Proverbs | Prov. | Pro | Proverbs |
| Ecc | Ecclesiastes | Eccl. | Ecc | Ecclesiastes |
| Sol | Song of Solomon | Cant. | Sol | Song |
| Isa | Isaiah | Isa. | Isa | Isaiah |
| Jer | Jeremiah | Jer. | Jer | Jeremiah |
| Lam | Lamentations | Lam. | Lam | Lamentations |
| Eze | Ezekiel | Ezek. | Eze | Ezekiel |
| Dan | Daniel | Dan. | Dan | Daniel |

| Hos | Hosea | Hos. | Hos | Hosea |
|---|---|---|---|---|
| Joe | Joel | Joel | Joe | Joel |
| Amo | Amos | Amos | Amo | Amos |
| Oba | Obadiah | Obad. | Oba | Obadiah |
| Jon | Jonah | Jon. | Jon | Jonah |
| Mic | Micah | Mic. | Mic | Micah |
| Nah | Nahum | Nah. | Nah | Nahum |
| Hab | Habakkuk | Hab. | Hab | Habakkuk |
| Zep | Zephaniah | Zeph. | Zep | Zephaniah |
| Hag | Haggai | Hag. | Hag | Haggai |
| Zec | Zechariah | Zech. | Zec | Zechariah |
| Mal | Malachi | Mal. | Mal | Malachi |
| Mat | Matthew | Matt. | Mat | Matthew |
| Mar | Mark | Mk. | Mar | Mark |
| Luk | Luke | Lk. | Luk | Luke |
| Joh | John | Jn. | Joh | John |
| Act | Acts | Acts | Act | Acts |
| Rom | Romans | Rom. | Rom | Romans |
| 1Co | 1 Corinthians | 1 Co. | 1Co | 1Corinthians |
| 2Co | 2 Corinthians | 2 Co. | 2Co | 2Corinthians |
| Gal | Galatians | Gal. | Gal | Galatians |
| Eph | Ephesians | Eph. | Eph | Ephesians |
| Phi | Philippians | Phil. | Phi | Philippians |
| Col | Colossians | Col. | Col | Colossians |
| 1Th | 1 Thessalonians | 1 Thess. | 1Th | 1Thessalonians |
| 2Th | 2 Thessalonians | 2 Thess. | 2Th | 2Thessalonians |
| 1Ti | 1 Timothy | 1 Tim. | 1Ti | 1Timothy |
| 2Ti | 2 Timothy | 2 Tim. | 2Ti | 2Timothy |
| Tit | Titus | Tit. | Tit | Titus |
| Phm | Philemon | Phlm. | Phm | Philemon |
| Heb | Hebrews | Heb. | Heb | Hebrews |
| Jam | James | Jas. | Jam | James |

| 1Pe | 1 Peter | 1 Pet. | 1Pe | 1Peter |
|---|---|---|---|---|
| 2Pe | 2 Peter | 2 Pet. | 2Pe | 2Peter |
| 1Jo | 1 John | 1 Jn. | 1Jo | 1John |
| 2Jo | 2 John | 2 Jn. | 2Jo | 2John |
| 3Jo | 3 John | 3 Jn. | 3Jo | 3John |
| Jud | Jude | Jude | Jud | Jude |
| Rev | Revelation | Rev. | Rev | Revelation |
| 1Es | 1 Esdras | 1 Es. | 1Es | 1Esdras |
| Jdt | Judith | Jdt. | Jdt | Judith |
| Tob | Tobit | Tob. | Tob | Tobit |
| 1Ma | 1 Maccabees | 1 Ma. | 1Ma | 1Maccabees |
| 2Ma | 2 Maccabees | 2 Ma. | 2Ma | 2Maccabees |
| 3Ma | 3 Maccabees | 3 Ma. | 3Ma | 3Maccabees |
| 4Ma | 4 Maccabees | 4 ma. | 4Ma | 4Maccabees |
| Ode | Odes | Odes | Ode | Odes |
| Wis | Wisdom | Wis. | Wis | Wisdom |
| Sir | Sirach | Sir. | Sir | Sirach |
| Sip | Sip | Sip | Sip | Sip |
| Pss | Psalms of Solomon | Ps. Sol. | Pss | |
| Bar | Baruch | Bar. | Bar | Baruch |
| Epj | Epistle of Jeremiah | Ep. Jer. | Epj | |
| Sus | Susanna | Sus. | Sus | Susanna |
| Bel | Bel | Bel. | Bel | Bel |
| Pra | Prayer of Azariah | Pr. Az. | Pra | Azariah |
| Dng | Daniel (Greek) | Dng | Dng | Dng |
| Prm | Prayer of Manasseh | Pr. Man. | Prm | Manasseh |
| Psx | Psalm(151) | Psx. | Psx | |
| Lao | Laodiceans | Lao. | Lao | Laodiceans |
| 4Es | 4 Esdras | 4 Es. | 4Es | 4Esdras |
| Esg | Esther (Greek) | Esg. | Esg | |
| Jsa | Joshua (A) | Jsa. | Jsa | |

| Jda | Judges (A) | Jda. | Jda | |
|---|---|---|---|---|
| Tbs | Tobit (S) | Tbs. | Tbs | |
| Sut | Susanna (TH) | Sut. | Sut | |
| Dat | Daniel (TH) | Dat. | Dat | |
| Bet | Bel (TH) | Bet. | Bet | |
| WCF | WCF | WCF | WCF | |
| WLC | WLC | WLC | WLC | |
| WSC | WSC | WSC | WSC | |

# THE BOOK OF THE WATCHERS CHAPTERS 17-36

## The Journey Narrative Begun

17:1 And they took me (and) led (me) away to a certain place in which those who were there were like a flaming fire; and whenever they wished, they appeared as human beings. 2 And they led me away to a dark place and to a mountain whose summit reached to heaven. 3 And I saw the place of the luminaries and the treasuries of the stars and of the thunders, and to the depths of the ether, where the bow of fire and the arrows and their quivers (were) and the sword of fire 5and all the lightnings. 4 And they led me away to the living waters and to the fire of the west, which provides all the sunsets. 5 And I came to the river of fire, in which fire flows down like water and discharges into the great sea of the west. 6 I saw all the great rivers. And I arrived at the great river and the great darkness. And I departed (for) where no human walks. 7 I saw the wintry winds of darkness and the gushing of all the waters of the abyss. 8 I saw the mouth of all the rivers of the earth and the mouth of abyss.

Special Note: the journey of Enoch is like the Epic of Gilgamesh.[i]

Questioning the Narrative

1. Who are the creatures of verse one?

   The "creatures" are angels who took Enoch back into Heaven as a part of his journey.

2. Where is a "certain place" in verse one?

   A certain place is a vague term which could have been used to keep the reader interested in continuing to read the story.

3. Why could they appear as human beings? (v. 1)

   It is known that angels can become humans (as shown when the Watchers came to Earth). The angels become human so that Enoch can understand them.

4. Is there a purpose to the creatures in verse one?

   The angels are to escort Enoch through Heaven.

5. Why are the creatures described as a flaming fire? (v. 1)

   The flaming fire could be a sign of the Chasmal angels (refer to Dr. Koplitz's book, "Understanding Ezekiel" chapter one). This could be Enoch's way of describing the glow that he saw in material terms.

6. If Enoch is in heaven, why is there a mountain that reaches Heaven described? (v. 2)

   The mountain is reaching Heaven shows Enoch is on Earth when this angelic encounter occurs.

7. What is the dark place? (v. 2)

   The dark place could be Hell. If so, Enoch went through hell before going to Heaven. However, the Pit, which is hell, is sealed shut containing Azazel. The dark place could be a place that Enoch cannot explain in human terms. The dark place could be a place that allowed Enoch to see the Luminaries. It could be awaiting area, a lobby, and then the "tunnel" would go to Heaven.

8. Why are the words luminaries and stars using in verse three since they are synonyms?

   The author may point out that there is a difference between stars.

9. What are the treasuries of thunder? (v. 3)

   This is the place of the origin of thunder. Ancient cosmology did not understand that thunder is a sound produced by lightning.

10. What is living water? (v. 4)

    The biblical definition is water that is flowing and is pure for drinking because it is always moving. It allegorically means lasting life.

11. Is the fire in the west the sun we know today? (v. 4)

    This is where the sunsets end up. Fire means purification. The sun provides heat for purification. The sun releases its purification during the day and then recharges itself in the west.

12. Does the wording of verse four show a time frame?

    It is not defined.

13. What is the river of fire? (v. 5)

    The river of fire could be from Daniel 7:10. It is possible that the river of fire recharges the sun. The river of fire could flow under the Earth to recharge the sun.

14. What is the great sea in the west? (v. 5)

    This is the Mediterranean Sea. It is possibly another sea, but most likely the Mediterranean.

15. Is the living water the same as the great sea? (v. 5)

    The living water flows into the sea from rivers. The water in the great sea would be salty while the rivers were not. The rivers eventually feed into the great sea.

16. Is there a specific place in the west that Enoch was taken? (v. 5)

    It is not specified.

17. Do all the great rivers flow into the great sea in the west? (v. 6)

    There is none specified. All rivers flow into a sea or an ocean.

18. Which great river did Enoch arrive at? (v. 6)

    This is not specified.

19. What are the great rivers? (v. 6)

    It is possibly the four great rivers of the Bible: Tigris, Euphrates, Gihon and Psion rivers.

20. Can the great sea drain into the great rivers? (v. 6)

    Since the sea of Galilee flows into the Jordan river, then the answer is yes.

21. Where is where no human walks? (v. 6)

    This could be heaven because flesh cannot exist in heaven. It could be a place on Earth where no human has been yet.

22. What is the great darkness? (v. 6)

    This could be the end of the world where it was believed there was a void.

23. What are the wintry winds of darkness? (v. 7)

    Winds probably commence at the top of the mountain. It then descends downloads and the air is cold because of the evaluation.

24. If it is dark how can Enoch see it? (v. 7)

    Angels could glow, like the chasmal. You do not need light to see the wind.

25. What does the word "mouth" mean in verse eight? (v. 8)

    It is allegorical for an opening. It could be the start of all the rivers of the Earth.

26. Is this the only river in heaven? (v. 8)

    Seven rivers originate in Heaven.

27. Did Enoch have the special abilities to see these things? (general question)

    Since Enoch was in Heaven, he would have to can see things. This implies that there are things in Heaven that can be hidden from human sight. This could be metaphorical that Enoch could interpret everything He saw in Heaven.

28. Where is Enoch in verse eight?

    Enoch returned to Earth because he did not have angels with him.

## A Digression: A Summary of What Enoch Saw

18:1 I saw the treasuries of all the winds. I saw how through them he ordered all created things 2 I saw the foundation of the earth and the cornerstone of the earth. I saw the four winds bearing the earth and the firmament of heaven. 3 And I saw how the winds stretch out the height of heaven. They stand between earth and heaven; they are the pillars of heaven. 4 I saw the winds of heaven that turn and bring to (their) setting the disk of the sun and all the stars. 5 I saw the winds on the earth bearing the clouds. I saw the paths of the angels. I saw at the ends of the earth the firmament of heaven above.

### Linguistic Structure

**[I saw repetition]** 18:1 I saw the treasuries of all the winds.

**[I saw repetition]** I saw all created things.

**[I saw repetition]** I saw the four winds bearing the earth and the firmament of heaven.

**[I saw repetition]** 3 And I saw how the winds stretch out the height of heaven. They stand between earth and heaven; they are the pillars of heaven.

**[I saw repetition]** 4 I saw the winds of heaven that turn and bring to (their) setting the disk of the sun and all the stars.

**[I saw repetition]** 5 I saw the winds on the earth bearing the clouds

**[I saw repetition]** I saw the paths of the angels.

**[I saw repetition]** I saw at the ends of the earth the firmament of heaven above.

### Questioning the Narrative

1. Is the reference to "through the winds created all things" a reference to Genesis 1? (v. 1)

   Genesis 1 says that the Word of the LORD through the *ruach* (spirit) was upon the void and creation came from the Word. *Ruach* can also be translated as "wind." Therefore, the verse could be read as "through the Spirit of the LORD created all things."

2. What is the cornerstone of the Earth? (v. 2)
   Could the cornerstone of the Earth be in the center of the Earth? The foundation is the center because ancient people visualized the Earth as a flat disc.

3. What is the Foundation of the Earth? (v. 2)
   The foundation of the Earth was the pillars of stone that kept the Earth from sinking into the underground river which flowed below the Earth.

4. Are the four winds equal to the compass points? (v. 2)
   The four winds of the Earth correspond to the four corners of the world, which are the four compass points.

5. What does "winds stretch out the heights of Heaven" mean? (v. 3)
   The "heights of Heaven" is the distance between the firmament and Heaven. The firmament is the barrier which separates Heaven and Earth.

6. Could verse three be the definition of the layers of Heaven? (v. 3)
   Yes.

7. Why does heaven need pillars? (v. 3)
   In the days of this writing, the people believed in cosmology that everything, including heaven, needed pillars to support it.

8. Do the winds of Earth cause day and night? (v. 4)

   This is another idea about the movement of the sun and the moon. In an earlier chapter of 1 Enoch, it was discovered that the sun and moon are sitting in chariots which are pulled around the sky. In this chapter, the winds are believed to push the sun and moon around the sky.

9. What is the path of the angels? (v. 5)

   This is an illusion of Jacob's ladder, which can be found in Genesis.

10. Do all angels follow the path? (v. 5)

    This verse shows one path for angels. Also, in Jacob's ladder, the angels went up and down the ladder to reach Heaven and Earth.

11. What are the ends of the Earth? (v. 5)

    Enoch determined what he thought the ends of the Earth were after being taken there by the angels. The end of the Earth would be where the Earth and firmament touch.

12. Where was Enoch at this time?

    Since Enoch was experiencing a vision, he was probably in a trance. Another view is that his soul was taken up to Heaven.

13. Is there a void area between Heaven and Earth?

    It was believed that there was.

14. How long did the journey take (is there time in heaven)?

    Since it is believed that time is a creation of the physical universe, then it is unknown how long Enoch's journey was. It is believed that time does not exist in the heavenly realm.

## The Journey Narrative Concluded

6 I came and saw a place that was burning night and day, where (there were) seven mountains of precious stones—three lying to the east and three to the south. 7 And of those to the east, (one was) of colored stone, and one was of pearl, and one was of <jasper>. And those to the south were of flame-colored stone. 8/ And the middle one of them reached to heaven like the throne of God—of antimony; and the top of the throne was of lapis lazuli. 9 And I saw a burning fire. 10 And beyond these mountains is a place, the edge of the great earth; there the heavens come to an end. 11 And I saw a great chasm among pillars of heavenly fire. And I saw in it pillars of fire descending; and they were immeasurable toward the depth and toward the height.

19:1 And Uriel said to me, "There stand the angels who mingled with the women. And their spirits—having assumed many forms—bring destruction on men and lead them astray to sacrifice to demons as to gods until the day of the great judgment, in which they will be judged with finality. 2 And the wives of the transgressing angels will become sirens."

12 Beyond this chasm I saw a place where there was neither firmament of heaven above, nor firmly founded earth beneath it. Neither was there water on it, nor bird; but the place was desolate and fearful. 13 There I saw seven stars like great burning mountains. 14 To me, when I inquired about them, the angel said, "This place is the end of heaven and earth; this has become a prison for the stars and the hosts of heaven. 15/ The stars that are rolling over in the fire, these are they that transgressed the command of the Lord in the in the beginning of their rising, for they did not come out in their appointed times. 16 And he was angry with them and bound them until the time of the consummation of their sins – ten thousand years.

19:3 I, Enoch alone saw the visions, the extremities of all things. And no one among humans has seen as I saw.

Linguistic Structure

V. 6-11 "I saw" repetition

V. 6 repetition of night and day

V. 9 repetition of the burning fire

V. 10-11 repetition of the Pillars of Fire

Questioning the narrative

1. Is there a description or note of the seventh mountain (v. 6)

   A full description of the mountains is not in the text. It is possible that the middle mountain is the Mountain of God. That would mean that Mount Sinai is on Earth and extends into Heaven. If so, then the Exodus passage about Moses ascending the mountain of Sinai works since Moses never reached the very top of the mountain because the top of the mountain is in heaven.

2. What is the significance of the stones? (v. 7)

   A pearl is not polished nor cut by man. It is white and thus signifies purity because of its color, and that needs nothing done to it to be round and smooth. Jasper is usually cut in a triangular shape, signifying the number three, which is a sign of the divine. Antimony is a white stone signifying purity. The unidentified colored stone could be diamonds.

3. Is there a border around heaven? (v. 7)

   There are gates into heaven showing a border. Also, there is a firmament which separates heaven and earth. Therefore, there must be a border.

4. Can Enoch see where the watchers are imprisoned? (v. 19:1)

   Ariel indicates to Enoch that from the place in Heaven they were in that the imprisoned Watchers are inside the foundation of the Earth.

5. What forms did they (the Watchers) take? (v. 19:1)

   The Watchers were in a form which enabled them to exist inside of the foundations of the Earth. A description of them is not offered in the text.

6. Who are the demons mentioned in verse 19:1?

   The Gospels of Jesus Christ says that Jesus exorcised the Watchers who had infected humans. Also, Jesus caused the demons to be sent to Hell to join Aziel.

7. What are sirens? (v. 19:2)

   Sirens are part woman and part bird. Sirens in Greek mythology would fly past ships on the sea and got the sailors to jump into the sea. Therefore, the siren was known as a creature which lures sailors to their death.

   From "Sirens" in the Book of Enoch? By James Scott Trimm
   In the Book of Enoch, we read:
   "And the women also of the angels who went astray shall become ***sirens***." (1Enoch 19:2).

   Although the Ethiopic text has "*salamaweyan*" ("peaceful") which is widely regarded as corruption with the original reading being that found in the Greek εις σειρηνας "into sirens." This is certainly a passage which we would like to see in the Aramaic, much less the original lost Hebrew, but unfortunately, the Aramaic for this passage has not survived.

   In Greek mythology, the Sirens were beautiful yet dangerous creatures, who lured nearby sailors with their enchanting music and voices to shipwreck on the rocky coast of their island. So why would the Book of Enoch refer to "sirens". Why would an ancient Hebrew text refer to "sirens" and what was the original Hebrew word(s) behind "sirens"?[23]

[23] James Trimm, "'Sirens' in the Book of Enoch?," Nazarene Space, accessed July 16, 2019, http://nazarenespace.ning.com/profiles/blogs/sirens-in-the-book-of-enoch.

8. Why are verses 18:12-14 moved inside the chapter?

   This passage is parallel to 19:1-2, which makes a chiastic repetition. The commentary in the text is from the author.

9. What is beyond the chasm? (v. 18:12)

   This could refer to a "void" where the LORD could reside.

10. Why was the place described as fearful? (v. 8:12)

    Because this place was empty of life, water and was unfamiliar, therefore it was frightening to enter it.

11. What are the seven stars? (v. 8:13)

    This could be a reference to the Pleiades. This constellation was well known in Greek times with several legends about the seven stars. It could also be a reference to the seven days of creation.

12. What is the simile for "great burning mountains? (v. 18:13)

    This could be a prison, a place of confinement where the stars and host of heaven are confined. It was believed that stars and angels could not be destroyed. Therefore, the LORD needed a place to put the ones who transgress.

13. Is there a prison in Heaven? (v. 18:14)

    Enoch describes a "holding" area for the stars that disobeyed the LORD. This area is called a prison. Therefore, the answer is "yes."

14. Why are the stars and angels placed in prison? (v. 18:14)

    The stars and angels who disobey the LORD are placed in prison.

15. Is the prison on Earth? (v. 18:14)

    Enoch is on his journey through Heaven. It is logical to assume that the prison that he is describing is in Heaven.

16. Do stars have free will? (v. 18:15)

    Since the stars can disobey the LORD by not coming out at their designated times, it can be assumed that the stars have free will.

17. What does "stars are rolling in the fire" mean? (v. 18:15)

    Stars are being on fire because fire creates light. Therefore, stars must have a fire on them. Another idea is that they are being punished with fire.

18. What is the appointed time? (v. 18:15)

    This is the designated time the LORD wants a star to appear in the sky.

19. Could the stars be a metaphor and, if so, for what? (v. 18:15)

    The stars are a part of heaven. Since they can disobey the LORD, they seem to have similar properties as angels.

20. Why is the time frame showed as 10,000 years in verse 18:16?

    The number of 10,000 is symbolic of eternity. It can also show the number of years between the creation of Heaven and Earth and judgment day. Remember that a day to the LORD is 1,000 years on Earth.

## Enoch's Journey Eastward (Chapters 20–36)

### The list of the Seven Archangels

20:1 These are the names of the holy angels who watch. 2 Uriel, one of the holy angels, who is in charge of the world and Tartarus. 3 Raphael, one of the holy angels, who is in charge of the spirits of men. 4 Reuel, one of the holy angels, who takes vengeance on the world of the luminaries. 5 Michael, one of the holy angels, who has been put in charge of the good one of the people. 6 Sariel, one of the holy angels, who is in charge of the spirits who sin against the spirit. 7 Gabriel, one of the holy angels, who is in charge of paradise and the serpents and the cherubim. 8 Remiel, one of the holy angels, whom God has put in charge of them that rise. The names of the seven archangels.

1. Uriel is in charge of all angels.
2. Raphael is in charge of healing.
3. Reuel is in charge of the final judgment.
4. Michael is the patron of righteousness.
5. Sariel is the LORD's messenger to Noah.
6. Gabriel is the guardian of paradise and its guardians.
7. Remiel is in charge of resurrections.

## The Place of Punishment for the Disobedient Stars

21:1 I traveled to where it was chaotic. 2 And there I saw a terrible thing; I saw neither heaven above, nor firmly founded earth, but a chaotic and terrible place. 3 And there I saw seven of the stars of heaven, bound and thrown in it together, like great mountains, and burning in fire. 4 Then I said, "For what reason have they been bound, and for what reason have they been thrown here?" 5 Then Uriel said to me, one of the holy angels who was with me, and he was their leader, he said to me, "Enoch, why do you inquire, and why are you eager for the truth?

6 These are the stars of heaven that transgressed the command of the Lord; they have been bound here until ten thousand years are fulfilled—the time of their sins." The Prison of the Fallen Angels 7 From there I traveled to another place, more terrible than this one. And I saw terrible things—a great fire burning and flaming there. And the place had a narrow cleft (extending) to the abyss, full of great pillars of fire, borne downward. Neither the measure nor the size was I able to see or to estimate. 8 Then I said, "How terrible is this place and fearful to look at!" 9 Then Uriel answered me, one of the holy angels who was with me, and said to me, "Enoch, why are you so frightened and shaken?" A I replied "Because of this terrible place and because of the fearful sight." 10 And he said, "This place is a prison for the angels. Here they will be confined forever."

Questioning the narrative

1. Why are there only seven stars in heaven and seven mountains? (v. 3)

   There are more than seven stars in heaven. Number seven is the key. It is the number which symbolizes the completeness of creation.

2. How can stars be bound?

   The method of bounding a star is not described.

3. Do angels have genders?

   Angels do not have genders in the same sense as humans have genders. However, the characteristic of being male or female exists in angels. When angels come to Earth and take human form, they can be male or female, as shown in the first part of the Book of the Watchers and Genesis chapter six.

4. Is Uriel always the leader of the angels?

   In this part of the Enoch legend, Uriel is the leader of the angels. That does not mean that Uriel will always be the leader of the angels.

5. Can stars have free will?

   The answer to this question at this point in the narrative is "yes." This can be seen in the wandering stars (the planets) which appear as the ability to determine their direction.

6. How can the great pillars of fire be borne downward?

   Perhaps the great pillars of fire are coal deposits that are on fire, and the fire started at the top of the coal deposit and worked its way downward. Perhaps this is a solar flare that Enoch is seeing. The flare emits from the sun's surface then returns, usually in an arch, which would look like a great pillar of fire that moves downward. The fire could be a barrier to keeping the angels in their confinement.

7. Why does verse seven say "measure nor the size?"

   Since Enoch cannot see the end of the area, it appears to be infinite in his eyes.

8. What is the narrow cleft? (v. 7)

   This is an observation deck from which Enoch can make his observations.

9. Who is Enoch speaking to in verse eight?

   Enoch is speaking to the angel Uriel.

10. How many holy angels are with Enoch? (v. 9)

    The text says a group of angels was with Enoch. The exact number is unknown.

11. Why was Enoch frightened and shaken? (v. 9)

    Enoch was scared for his life, which is interesting since he was in Heaven. Perhaps it was a feeling of hopelessness. Seeing a prison in heaven for the angels may have made him contemplate if there could be a prison for human spirits in Heaven.

12. Why is Hell a part of the tour of Heaven? (v. 9)

    Since Enoch wrote the book as a warning to his children, he wanted them to know that there is a consequence for their disobedience to the Laws of the LORD.

13. Is this a place only for angels? (v. 10)

    Yes.

## The Mountain of the Dead

22:1 From there I traveled to another place. And he showed me to the west a great and high mountain of hard rock. 2 And there were four hollow places in it, deep and very smooth. Three of them were dark and one, illuminated; and a fountain of water was in the middle of it. And I said, "How smooth are these hollows and altogether deep and dark to view." 3 Then Raphael answered me, one of the holy angels who was with me, and said to me, "These hollow places (are intended) that the spirits of the souls of the dead might be gathered into them. For this very (purpose) they were created, (that) here the souls of all human beings should be gathered. 4 And look, these are the pits for the place of their confinement. Thus they were made until the day (on) which they will be judged, and until the time of the day of the end of the great judgment that will be exacted from them." 5 There I saw the spirit of a dead man making suit, and his lamentation went up to heaven and cried and made suit. 6 Then I asked Raphael, the watcher and holy one who was with me, and said to him, "This spirit that makes suit—whose is it—that thus his lamentation goes up and makes suit unto heaven?" 7 And he answered me and said, "This is the spirit that went forth from Abel, whom Cain his brother murdered. And Abel makes accusation against him until his posterity perishes from the face of the earth, and his posterity is obliterated from the posterity of men." 8 Then I asked about all the hollow places, why they were separated one from the other. 9 And he answered me and said, "These three were made that the spirits of the dead might be separated. And this has been separated for the spirits of the righteous, where the bright fountain of water is. 10 And this has been created for <the spirits of the> sinners, when they die and are buried in the earth, and judgment has not been executed on them in their life. 11 Here their spirits are separated for this great torment, until the great day of judgment, of scourges and tortures of the cursed forever, that there might be a recompense for their spirits. There he will bind them forever. 12 And this has been separated for the spirits of them that make suit, who make decisions about the destruction, when they were murdered in the days of the sinners. 13 And this was created for the spirits of the people who will not be pious, but sinners, who were godless, and they were companions with the lawless. And their spirits will not be punished on the day of judgment, nor will they be raised from there." 14 Then I blessed the Lord of glory and said, "Blessed is the judgment of righteousness and blessed are you, O Lord of majesty and righteousness, who are Lord for eternity.

Linguistic Structure

22:1 – repetition - very smooth, hollow places

22:3 – repetition - souls gathered, darkness

22:5 – repetition - Suit

22:8 – repetition - hollow places—also in v. 10, 13, 14

22:3 – repetition - Judgment/judges

22:7 – repetition - Posterity

Questioning the narrative

1. Why are there smooth walls in the hollow places? (v. 2)
   A possibility is that one cannot climb out of the hollow places if the walls are smooth. That raises the question, do spirits have some kind of human body? If these are spirits, what prevents them from "flying" out?

2. Why is one illuminated? (v. 2)
   This is the place for the righteous. The illumination could be the righteousness of the spirits in this place. They are filled with the Light of the LORD.

3. Why are three dark hollow places, and one is illuminated? (v. 2)
   The three dark, hollow places are for the unrighteous, and one illuminated place is for the righteous. An interesting question is "who determines which hollow a spirit is placed in?" Raphael is in charge of the spirits of humans; therefore, he makes the determination.

4. What is the significance of water? (v. 2)
   It could be a metaphor for wisdom, cleanliness, or living water. Did the fountain reach to Heaven? The passage does not give any indication one way or the other. What Enoch thought was that water could be beams of Light.

5. Where is the fountain of water located? (v. 2)
   The fountain is in the illuminated hollow.

6. Why is Raphael answering Enoch? (v. 3)
   Raphael is in charge of the spirits of humans. Therefore, it is correct for Raphael to be there answering Enoch's questions.

7. What is the location of the Mountain of the dead?

> "It is situated in Siwa oasis. The mountain contains number of tombs. The tombs, which cover every inch of its base and are situated on its terraces and on all sides of the conical part, date from the 26th dynasty, the Greek and the Roman periods, though there appear to be no Christian burials.
>
> One of the most famous tombs is that of Si-Amun, which is considered the most beautiful one in the oasis of the Western desert. The tomb dates to about the 3rd century BC. It was discovered in October,1940 and unfortunately, some of its decorations were badly damaged by soldiers in Siwa at that time, who cut away parts of the painted plaster. The tomb, as with others in the area, was robbed during the Roman period."[24]

[24] "Mountain of the Dead in Siwa | Gebel Al-Mawta." Memphis Tours. Accessed October 12, 2018. https://www.memphistours.com/Egypt/WikiTravel/the-western-desert-and-oases/wiki/Mountain-of-the-Dead.

8. Is the mountain of the dead the place where the LORD's judgment will take place?

   This is a logical place to hold judgment because all the spirits of humankind are there.

9. How are the sinners confined to the pit? (v. 4)

   The walls in the hollows that the sinners live in are smooth walls. This prevents the sinners from climbing out of the hollows.

10. What does it mean "to take suit?" (v. 4)

    "Making suit" means petitioning for justice.

11. Is there a time that the hollows expire? (v. 4)

    The hollows will exist until the Day of Judgment. When the Day of Judgment comes, the LORD will judge the sinners. A decision is then made whether the person gets to be in Heaven or is sent to Hell. Also, on the Day of Judgment, the physical world ends. Therefore, there would be no more people born who would need to be eventually judged. The hollows will not be needed after the Day of Judgment.

12. Can the spirit repent of sins in order to come out of the pits? (v. 5)

    It is possible that the hollows are a place for the sinners to repent from their sins. Then when judgment day comes, their repentance could allow the LORD to offer forgiveness.

13. Is verse five indicating that the mountain is not in heaven ("suit into heaven")? (v. 6)

    Verse five does not say if the Mountain of the Dead is in Heaven or not. Since Enoch is touring Heaven, the logical assumption is that he sees what is in Heaven. Could there be a void between the firmament of Earth and Heaven where the Mountain of the Dead could exist? If so, then Enoch is seeing what is happening "under" heaven. The Mountain of the Dead outside of Heaven is logical because the Scripture says that sinners do not get to Heaven. If the Mountain of the Dead is inside of Heaven, then sinners would go to Heaven in order to be placed in the proper hollow.

14. Who separates the souls into each pit?

    The text says that Raphael is in charge of the hollows. Therefore, he would determine which pits each person is placed in.

15. Why are the hollow places separated from each other? (v. 8)

    The hollows are separated from each other because each hollow has a different purpose, and the souls in each are not supposed to intermingle.

16. Would Cain's offspring be separated from others? (v. 9)

    It was believed that the sin of the father is passed down to the children. If this is true, then all of Cain's offspring would be held in one sinner hollows.

17. Why are there three dark hollow places? (v. 9)

    Darkness is equated to sin, while the light is equated to righteous. The dark hollows were for the sinner. The sinners are divided into three groups based on what their sins were.

18. What judgment is being referred to in verse ten?

    This reference is to the final judgment, which will happen on the Day of Judgment.

19. Why is there division for sinners? (v. 1)

    This shows that there are "levels" to sin. Levels to sin can be found in Leviticus because there are different sacrifices are required to be forgiven.

20. What does "make disclosure about destruction" mean in verse 12?

    The future is being revealed so that sinners can decide to make amends before they die.

Hollow places of the Mountain of the Dead

| MURDERED | RIGHTEOUS (light) |
| --- | --- |
| NOT PIOUS | SINNERS |

## The Fire of the West

23:1 And from there I traveled to another place, to the west of the ends of the earth.
2 And I saw a fire that ran and did not rest or quit its course day and night, but
continued. 3 And I asked and said, "What is this that has no rest?" 4 Then Reuel
answered me, one of the holy angels who was with me, and said to me, "This course of
fire is the fire of the west, which pursues all the luminaries of heaven" 24:1 And he
showed me mountains of fire that burned day and night.

1. What is the significance of the fire? (v. 1)

   The following verses also refer to fire: 14:9-10, 14:12, 14:19, 17:4-5, 18:15. The description of the fire could lead one to believe that it is a river of fire. Could the river of fire be a barrier between Heaven and the Throne room of the LORD? The text said earlier that there is a firmament between Heaven and the Throne room and could be viewed as a separation of heaven and the throne of the LORD. The makeup of the firmament is not defined.

   The view of the fire is that it is an inherent tool that is a part of man. "The Hebrew word for fire is אש (*esh*). Derived from this two-letter parent root is the three-letter child root איש (*iysh*) meaning "man". Not only are these two words related by their letters, they are also related in meaning."[25]

2. Why does the "river of fire not quit" mean? (v. 2)

   The river does not quit and acts as if it is looking for something.

3. How long was Enoch there observing the fire?

   There is no indication in the text about this question.

[25] The Culture of the Hebrew Language. Accessed January 15, 2019. http://www.ancient-hebrew.org/articles_fire.html.

4. Why does the river pursue the luminaries?

   It was believed that the luminaries were "balls of fire." Therefore, the luminaries would attract fire so that they can maintain their brightness. Enoch could observe the Milky Way galaxy arms.

5. What are the mountains of fire? (v. 24.1)

   It appeared to Enoch that the tops of these mountains were on fire constantly.

## The Mountain of God and the Tree of Life

24:2 And I proceeded beyond them, and I saw seven glorious mountains, all differing each from the other, whose stones were precious in beauty. And all (the mountains) were precious and glorious and beautiful in appearance—three to the east were firmly set one on the other, and three to the south, one on the other, and deep and rugged ravines, one not approaching the other. 3/ The seventh mountain (was) in the middle of these, and it rose above them in height, like the seat of a throne. And fragrant trees encircled it. 4/ Among them was a tree such as I had never smelled, and among them was no other like it. It had a fragrance sweeter smelling than all spices, and its leaves and its blossom and the tree never wither. Its fruit is beautiful, like dates of the palm trees. 5 Then I said, "How beautiful is this tree and fragrant,[69] and its leaves are lovely, and its blossoms[70] are lovely to look at." 6 Then Michael answered me, one of the holy angels who was with me and was their leaders, 25:1/ and he said to me, "Enoch, why do you inquire and why do you marvel about the fragrance of this tree, and why do you wish to learn the truth?" 25:2 Then I answered him – I, Enoch – and said, "Concerning all things I wish to know, but especially concerning this tree." 3 And he answered me and said, "This high mountain that you saw, whose peak is like the throne of God, is the seat where the Great Holy One, the Lord of glory, the King of eternity, will sit, when he descends to visit the earth in goodness. 4/ And (as for) this fragrant tree, no flesh has the right to touch it until the great judgment, in which there will be vengeance on all and a consummation forever. Then it will be given to the righteous and the pious, 5 and its fruit will be food for the chosen. And it will be transplanted to the holy place, by the house of God, the King of eternity. 6 Then they will rejoice greatly and be glad, and they will enter into the sanctuary. Its fragrances <will be> in their bones, and they will live a long life on the earth, such as your fathers lived also in their days, and torments and plagues and suffering will not touch them." 7 Then I blessed the God of glory, the King of eternity, who has prepared such things for people (who are) righteous, and has created them and promised to give (them) to them.

Linguistic Structure

24:2-5 is an expansion of 18:6-9 using the rules of Hillel

24:2-3 describes the seven mountains

24:5 Enoch questions the one tree

24:6 Michael gives an answer to the question

25:6-7 Description of the tree

Questioning the Passage

1. Can a spiritual being touch the tree? (v. 25:4)

   The answer to this question is based on whether Enoch is in heaven or on Earth. Perhaps Enoch has traveled from Heaven to Earth because verse 26:1 says, "center of the Earth." Perhaps the mountain descends from Heaven to Earth. Therefore, the top of the mountain would be in Heaven while the foundation be on the Earth.

2. How can the LORD descend from a mountain?

   The LORD can descend from His mountain. This can be found in Exodus.

3. Why is the seventh mountain described as the seat of the LORD's throne? (v. 24:3)

   It was believed that the throne of God was at the top of the seventh mountain. Therefore, this mountain had to be the highest one.

4. How could Enoch see the mountain was encircled by trees? (v. 24:3)

   Enoch could be seeing an aerial view of the mountain. Another possibility is that Enoch walked around the entire region of the seven mountains.

5. Why does Michael show Enoch the mountains? (v. 24:6)

   The mountains were important to Michael, so he showed them to Enoch. Perhaps the importance was because the throne of God was on the top of the seventh mountain.

6. Why does Enoch desire to know the truth? (v. 25:1)

   Enoch wanted to know everything he could about Heaven and was showing his desire to know the truth so that he could convey the information to the people of the Earth.

7. How would Enoch know that the blossoms never wither? (v. 24:4)

   This could be a reference showing that some time passed while Enoch was in the mountains.

8. What was the theology about the Tree of Life? (general question)

   The Tree of Life reference has been used in many areas of theology. The gift of life from the LORD comes from the Tree of Life.

9. What is a long life on Earth? (v. 25:6)

   Genesis chapter six shows that man can live up to 120 years.

10. Where did the transplanted tree end up? (v. 25:5)

    The Tree of Life will be transplanted when the new Temple comes from Heaven after the Day of Judgment. The fruit of the tree is for the righteous. The fruit is a metaphor for spiritual nourishment. The new Temple could remain in Heaven and thus can be accessed by all the righteous souls of time. It could be placed on a new Earth. The time after Judgment Day is not well known nor defined in Scripture or the Sacred writings.

11. How long was Enoch there, at the tree? (general question)

    It is unknown how long Enoch was at the tree.

12. How many angels were with Enoch? (general question)

At least four at this time. Uriel, Michael, Reuel, and Raphael are identified.

## CENTER OF THE EARTH

26:1 And from there I proceeded to the center of the earth, and I saw a blessed place where there were trees that had branches that abide and sprout. 2/ And there I saw a holy mountain. From beneath the mountain water (came) from the east, and it flowed toward the south. 3/ And I saw to the east another mountain higher than it, and between them a deep valley that had no breadth, and through it water was flowing beneath the mountain. 4/ And to the west of this, another mountain lower than it and not rising very high, and a deep and dry valley beneath it, between them, and another deep and dry valley, at the apex of the three mountains. 5/ And all the valleys were deep, of hard rock, and no tree was planted on them. 6/ And I marveled at the mountain, and I marveled at the valley, I marveled exceedingly. 27:1/ Then I said, "Why is this land blessed and all filled with trees, but this valley is cursed?" 2/ Then <Sariel> answered, one of the holy angels who was with me, and said to me, "This cursed valley is for those who are cursed forever. Here will be gathered all the cursed, who utter with their mouth an improper word against the Lord and speak hard things against his glory. Here they will be gathered, and here will be (their) habitation 3/ at the last times, in the days of righteous judgment in the presence of the righteous for all time. Here the godless will bless the Lord of glory, the King of eternity. 4/ In the days of their judgment they will bless in mercy in accordance with how he has apportioned to them." 5/ Then I blessed the Lord of glory, and his glory I made known and praised magnificently. To the Paradise of Righteousnes

Questioning the narrative

1. Why does the commentary title say that Jerusalem is the center of the Earth?
   In Hebraic literature, Jerusalem is considered the center of the Earth because the Temple of the LORD was located in this city. The tradition was very strong in the author's day.

2. Is there a connection between the mountain of the dead and the people in the valley?

The valley of the cursed people is where they will travel to after judgment day. The cursed are people who speak out against the LORD and follow pagan gods.

3. Is mercy possible to those in the valley?

   There appears to be a contradiction here. Nickelsburg says this is not understandable. Perhaps it is ironic because it may be possible to receive redemption.

4. How does one know a mountain is holy? (v. 26:2)

   The text states the mountain is holy. An angel told Enoch that the mountain was holy. That is how Enoch discovered it.

5. Why is water flowing from the east and not from the west? (v. 26:2)

   The text shows that water flowed from the east.

6. What is the distance from the blessed place to the blessed mountain?

   The distance is unknown and is not significant to the narrative.

7. What does it mean to be beneath the mountain? (v. 26:3)

   There was probably an underground river.

8. How can there be a valley at the apex of the mountain?

   The apex described could be a geological formation that was on the top of a mountain that gave this appearance.

9. Could one mountain be the mountain of the dead?

   Chapter 26:1 says that this mountain is not the mountain of the dead.

10. What does it mean to be cursed? (v. 27:2)
    
    Being cursed expresses a wish that misfortune, evil, and doom will befall on a person, thus disconnecting them from the LORD.

11. Is it possible that some of the cursed are already there and will be joined by more later?
    
    No, because the situation and place described followed judgment day. Curses must be directed before or on judgment day.

12. Why is the land blessed, but the valley is cursed? (v. 27:1)
    
    Evil had been invoked on the land. Being barren and dry is a sign of a cursed land. Not all barren land is cursed. The difference between a blessed place and a cursed place is that blessed spirits will live in the blessed land while cursed spirits live in cursed lands.

13. Why would people condemned to the cursed valley bless the LORD? (v. 27:4)
    
    Perhaps when they realize their evil ways, they tried to repent and plead to the LORD for forgiveness.

14. Can there be multiple places for Hell?
    
    From the descriptions in this section, sinful and cursed souls can end up in different locations. The Zohar says that there is Avadon and Sheol. In Avadon souls can repent of their sins and eventually leave Avadon for Heaven. Sheol is a place where sinful and cursed souls can never fully repent.

15. What is the function of the valley?

    The valley is for the cursed people who blaspheme against the LORD. It is a precursor to Hell.

16. What does "apportioning" mean? (v. 27:4)

    Apportioning in this context means giving different amounts to those who sin (it is like the Zohar concept of Avadon).

## TO THE PARADISE OF RIGHTEOUSNESS

28:1/ And from there I went to the midst of the mountain range of the desert. And I saw it was desolate, and it alone was full of trees <and plants>. 2/ Water was pouring forth from above. 3/ Flowing like a copious watercourse, approximately to the northwest, it brought water and also dew from all around. 29:1/ From there I went to another place in the desert, and I departed to the east of this mountain range. 2/ I saw trees <of the field> breathing fragrances of frankincense and myrrh, and their trees were like nut trees. 30:1/ Beyond these I departed far to the east. And I saw another vast place—valleys of water, 2/ in which were aromatic cane like reeds. 3/ On the banks of these valleys I saw the fragrant cinnamon. 31:1 Beyond these valleys, I departed to the east. And I saw other mountains, and also on them I saw trees, from which flowed the nectar called storax and galbanum. 2/ Beyond these mountains I was shown another mountain, and on it were aloe trees. All the trees were full of . . . . . . . . , and it was like the bark of the almond tree. 3/ When they grind this bark, it is sweeter than any perfume. 32:1/ Beyond these mountains, approximately to their northeastern side I saw other mountains, filled with choice nard and tspr and cardamom and pepper. 2/ From there I proceeded to the east of all these mountains, far from them to the east of the earth. And I passed over the Red Sea and departed far from it. And I crossed over the darkness, far from it. 3/ I passed by the paradise of righteousness, and I saw from afar trees more plentiful and larger than these trees, differing from those – very large <and> beautiful and glorious and magnificent—and the tree of wisdom, whose fruit the holy ones eat and learn great wisdom. 4/ That tree is in height like the fir, and its leaves, like (those of) the carob, and its fruit like the clusters of the vine—very cheerful; and its fragrance penetrates far beyond the tree. 5/ Then I said, "How beautiful is the tree and how pleasing in appearance." 6/ Then <Gabriel>,the holy angel who was with me, answered, "This is the tree of wisdom from which your father of old and your mother of old, who were before you, ate and learned wisdom. And their eyes were opened, and they knew that they were naked, and they were driven from the garden.

Questioning the narrative

1. Why would the dead need healing?

   Since it is the *ruach* (spirit) which rises to Heaven upon death, the healing is probably for those spirits who sinned while living upon the Earth.

2. Is there an oasis in the desert described? (v. 28:1-3)

   This might be a description of an oasis or simply a water source.

3. How can a range be desolate but also full of trees? (v. 28:1)

   The description of "desolate" could imply that there were no animals of any kind living in the area, that includes humans. However, there was a forest of trees.

4. What is the water source? (v. 28:2)

   The water source could be an oasis or a stream that flowed in that area.

5. Is the mountain range described in v. 29:1 the same as v 28:1?

   The text reads that there are two separate mountain ranges are being described. It is possible that the mountain range is one very large mountain range spanning across the territory.

6. Why is traveling to the east more plentiful? (v. 29:1-2; 30:1)

   As Enoch traveled eastward, he saw more in the mountains and valleys. When this book was written, the Hebrew people would look to the East because Jerusalem was on the eastern boundary next to the Jordan River. Prayer and worship were done pointing to Jerusalem (to the east, most times).

7. Were these lakes being described? (v. 30:1)

These were "valleys of water." It is possible that Enoch saw lakes. However, they could be rivers.

8. What is the source of the fragrances? (v. 29:1)

   Fragrances were derived from leaves, tree sap, and tree bark.

9. How did Enoch know that grinding the bark of the almond tree would be sweeter than perfumes? (v. 31:2)

   The text says, "like the bark of an almond tree." Enoch must have known what aloe trees smelled like (like almond).

10. What does "East of the Earth" mean? (v. 32:2-3)

    These two verses could describe the "tunnel" which many people who had near-death experiences describe. This would be the spiritual conduit between Earth and Heaven.

11. Where is the paradise of righteousness? (v. 32:3)

    The paradise appears to be in Heaven.

12. Is this place the Garden of Eden? (v. 32:3)

    It is believed that the paradise of righteousness is the Garden of Eden. There are Midrashim that say the Garden was in Heaven and when Adam and Eve sinned that the LORD had to remove them from the Garden, which removed them from Heaven. The LORD then placed them on the Earth.

13. Who can eat from the Tree of Wisdom? (v. 32:3)

    The text says that the Holy ones, who are angels of the LORD, could eat from the Tree of Wisdom.

## To the Ends of the Earth

33:1 And from there I proceeded to the ends of the earth, and I saw there great beasts, and they differed each from the other; and birds also, differing (in) their appearance and their beauty and their voices, differed each from the other. To the east of these beasts I saw the ends of the earth, on which the heaven rests, and the gates of heaven open. 2/ I saw how the stars of heaven come forth, and I counted the gates from which they emerge, 3/ and I wrote down all their outlets, one by one, according to their number and their names, according to their conjunction and their position and their time and their months, as Uriel, the holy angel who was with me, showed me. 4/ He should me and wrote down for me everything, and also he wrote down their names and their appointed times and their functions.

1. Why are there gates in Heaven? (v. 1)

   The Gates allow a human spirit to enter Heaven. It was believed that a firmament separated the Earth and Heaven. How would a human spirit enter Heaven unless there was a gate? Also, the angels of the LORD would have to leave Heaven to talk to humans.

2. What are the great beasts? (v. 1)

   The great beasts were animals that Enoch had never seen. There have been many species of animals that have inhabited the Earth. The animals that would be sent to the Earth later in history are living in Heaven (their spirits are).

3. What are the birds? (v. 1)

   The birds Enoch saw were probably birds that have not come to Earth yet.

4. What are the outlets? (v. 3)

   The outlets allow the luminaries to come out when it is their time to shine in the sky.

5. How did the angel Uriel write things down if there is no paper or other writing implements in Heaven? (v. 3)

   Language means that Uriel wrote everything described into Enoch's mind so that he could write it down when he returned to Earth.

6. What is the conjunction, their position, their time, and their months mean? (v. 3)

   The schedule for the luminaries is being described, which is expanded in the book of the Luminaries of 1 Enoch.

## Enoch's Journeys North, West, South, and East: A Summary

34:1/ And from there I proceeded to the north, at the ends of the earth, and there I saw great and glorious wonders at the ends of the whole earth. 2/ There I saw three gates of heaven open in heaven. From them the winds in the north emerge. When they blow, (there is) cold and hail and hoarfrost and snow and dew and rain. 3/ Through one gate they blow for good, and when they blow through two of the gates, they blow with violence, and there is affliction on the earth. 35:1/ From there I proceeded toward the west, at the ends of the earth, and I saw there three gates of heaven open, as I saw in the east, the same number of gates and the same number of outlets. 36:1 From there I proceeded toward the south, at the ends of the earth, and there I saw three gates of heaven open, and from there the south wind and dew and rain emerge. 2/ From there I proceeded toward the east, at the ends of the earth, and there I saw three gates of heaven open toward the east and above them, small gates. 3/ Through each of these small gates pass the stars of heaven, and they proceed westward on the path that is shown them. 4/ And when I saw, I blessed – I shall always bless – the Lord of glory, who was wrought great and glorious wonders to show his great deeds to his angels and to the spirits of human beings, so that they might see the work of his might and glorify the deeds

This is called a summary of what Enoch saw when he traveled through Heaven. What is described is that there are three gates at each corner of Heaven, north, south, east, and west. Above the gates are three smaller gates. The gates are for angels and human spirits to pass between Heaven and Earth. The smaller gates would allow the luminaries, the wind and the rain to pass from Heaven to Earth.

## BIBLIOGRAPHY

2016. "Aquinas." *Stanford Encyclopedia of Philosophy* on-line.

Borman, Throlief. 1960. *Hebrew Thought Compared with Greek.* Philadelphia, PA: Westminster Press.

Davis, Anne Kimball. 2015. *First Century Methods I: Recovering Ancient Methods of Bible Study.* Albuquerque, NM: Bibleinteract.

Davis, Anne Kimball. 2012. *The Synoptic Gospels.*

Dye, Diana. 2014. *Study to Show Yourself Approved.* Albuquerque, NM: Biblinteract.

n.d. *Epic of Gilgamesh.* Accessed March 1, 2018. http://www.sparknotes.com/lit/gilgamesh/summary/.

n.d. *Ethiopian Church Cannon.* Accessed January 24, 2018. http://www.ethiopianorthodox.org/english/canonical/books.html.

n.d. *Ethiopian Orthodox Church Bible.* Accessed January 24, 2018. http://www.ethiopianorthodox.org/english/canonical/books.html.

Fellman, Jack. 1973. *The Revival of a Classical Tongue.* Hague, Netherlands: Mouton.

n.d. *Gold as Money.* Accessed December 3, 2017. http://www.gold.org/history-and-facts/gold-money.

Howland, Jacob. 2011. *Plato and the Talmud.* Cambridge, England: Cambridge University Press.

Leven, Osher Chaim. 2013. *Jewish Wisdom in the Numbers.* Brooklyn, NY: Mesorah.

n.d. *Mountain of the Dead in Siwa.* Accessed October 12, 2018. https://www.memphistours.com/Egypt/WikiTravel/the-western-desert-and-oases/wiki/Mountain-of-the-Dead.

Nickelsburg, George W. E. 2001. *Hermeneia: A critical and historical commentary on the Bible - 1 Enoch.* Minneapolis, MN: Fortress Press.

—. 2012. *Hermenia: A modern translation of 1 Enoch.* Minneapolis, MN: Fortress Press.

1986. *Back to School.* Directed by Paper Clip Productions.

Roitman, Betty. 1998. *Black Fire on White Fire.* Berkeley, CA: University of Californmia Press.

n.d. *Testament of Levi.* Accessed February 14, 2017. https://en.wikipedia.org/wiki/Testaments_of_the_Twelve_Patriarchs.

n.d. *The Culture of the Hebrew Language.* Accessed January 15, 2019. http://www.ancient-hebrew.org/articles_fire.html.

n.d. *Tress and Bushes of the Holy Land.* Accessed August 06, 2016. http://www.biblewalks.com/info/Trees.html.

Trimm, J. 2000. *How to Understand the Scripture.* Hurst, TX: Society for the Advancement of Nazarene Judaism.

Trimm, James. n.d. *Sirens in the book of Enoch?* Accessed July 16, 2019. http://nazarenespace.ning.com/profiles/blogs/sirens-in-the-book-of-enoch.

Wilson, Marvin R. 1989. *Our Father Abraham.* Grand Rapids, MI: Eerdmans.

# END NOTES

---

[i] The epic's prelude offers a general introduction to Gilgamesh, king of Uruk, who was two-thirds god and one-third man. He built magnificent ziggurats, or temple towers, surrounded his city with high walls, and laid out its orchards and fields. He was physically beautiful, immensely strong, and very wise. Although Gilgamesh was godlike in body and mind, he began his kingship as a cruel despot. He lorded over his subjects, raping any woman who struck his fancy, whether she was the wife of one of his warriors or the daughter of a nobleman. He accomplished his building projects with forced labor, and his exhausted subjects groaned under his oppression. The gods heard his subjects' pleas and decided to keep Gilgamesh in check by creating a wild man named Enkidu, who was as magnificent as Gilgamesh. Enkidu became Gilgamesh's great friend, and Gilgamesh's heart was shattered when Enkidu died of an illness inflicted by the gods. Gilgamesh then traveled to the edge of the world and learned about the days before the deluge and other secrets of the gods, and he recorded them on stone tablets.

The epic begins with Enkidu. He lives with the animals, suckling at their breasts, grazing in the meadows, and drinking at their watering places. A hunter discovers him and sends a temple prostitute into the wilderness to tame him. In that time, people considered women and sex calming forces that could domesticate wild men like Enkidu and bring them into the civilized world. When Enkidu sleeps with the woman, the animals reject him since he is no longer one of them. Now, he is part of the human world. Then the harlot teaches him everything he needs to know to be a man. Enkidu is outraged by what he hears about Gilgamesh's excesses, so he travels to Uruk to challenge him. When he arrives, Gilgamesh is about to force his way into a bride's wedding chamber. Enkidu steps into the doorway and blocks his passage. The two men wrestle fiercely for a long time, and Gilgamesh finally prevails. After that, they become friends and set about looking for an adventure to share.

Gilgamesh and Enkidu decide to steal trees from a distant cedar forest forbidden to mortals. A terrifying demon named Humbaba, the devoted servant of Enlil, the god of earth, wind, and air, guards it. The two heroes make the perilous journey to the forest, and, standing side by side, fight with the monster. With assistance from Shamash the sun god, they kill him. Then they cut down the forbidden trees, fashion the tallest into an enormous gate, make the rest into a raft, and float on it back to Uruk. Upon their return, Ishtar, the goddess of love, is overcome with lust for Gilgamesh. Gilgamesh spurns her. Enraged, the goddess asks her father, Anu, the god of the sky, to send the Bull of Heaven to punish him. The bull comes down from the sky, bringing with him seven years of famine. Gilgamesh and Enkidu wrestle with the bull and kill it. The gods meet in council and agree that one of the two friends must be punished for their transgression, and they decide Enkidu is going to die. He takes ill, suffers immensely, and shares his visions of the underworld with Gilgamesh. When he finally dies, Gilgamesh is heartbroken.

Gilgamesh can't stop grieving for Enkidu, and he can't stop brooding about the prospect of his own death. Exchanging his kingly garments for animal skins as a way of mourning Enkidu, he sets off into the wilderness, determined to find Utnapishtim, the Mesopotamian Noah. After the flood, the gods had granted Utnapishtim eternal life, and Gilgamesh hopes that Utnapishtim can tell him how he might avoid death too. Gilgamesh's journey takes him to the twin-peaked mountain called Mashu, where the sun sets into one side of the mountain at night and rises out of the other side in the morning. Utnapishtim lives beyond the mountain, but the two scorpion monsters that guard its entrance refuse to allow Gilgamesh into the tunnel that passes through it. Gilgamesh pleads with them, and they relent.

After a harrowing passage through total darkness, Gilgamesh emerges into a beautiful garden by the sea. There he meets Siduri, a veiled tavern keeper, and tells her about his quest. She warns him that seeking immortality is futile and that he should be satisfied with the pleasures of this world. However, when she can't turn him away from his purpose, she directs him to Urshanabi, the ferryman. Urshanabi takes Gilgamesh on the boat journey across the sea and through the Waters of Death to Utnapishtim. Utnapishtim tells Gilgamesh the story of the flood—how the gods met in council and decided to destroy humankind. Ea, the god of wisdom, warned Utnapishtim about the gods' plans and told him how to fashion a gigantic boat in which his family and the seed of every living creature might escape. When the waters finally receded, the gods regretted what they'd done and agreed that they would never try to destroy humankind again. Utnapishtim was rewarded with eternal life. Men would die, but humankind would continue.

When Gilgamesh insists that he be allowed to live forever, Utnapishtim gives him a test. If you think you can stay alive for eternity, he says, surely you can stay awake for a week. Gilgamesh tries and immediately fails. So Utnapishtim orders him to clean himself up, put on his royal garments again, and return to Uruk where he belongs. Just as Gilgamesh is departing, however, Utnapishtim's wife convinces him to tell Gilgamesh about a miraculous plant that restores youth. Gilgamesh finds the plant and takes it with him, planning to share it with the elders of Uruk. But a snake steals the plant one night while they are camping. As the serpent slithers away, it sheds its skin and becomes young again.

When Gilgamesh returns to Uruk, he is empty-handed but reconciled at last to his mortality. He knows that he can't live forever but that humankind will. Now he sees that the city he had repudiated in his grief and terror is a magnificent, enduring achievement—the closest thing to immortality to which a mortal can aspire.

Source: http://www.sparknotes.com/lit/gilgamesh/summary/

www.ingramcontent.com/pod-product-compliance
Lightning Source LLC
LaVergne TN
LVHW080044170826
845677LV00024B/1600
*9798224331062*